W9-ACU-870

THE NEW BOOK OF

PHARAOHS

Dr. Anne Millard

Copper Beech Books
Brookfield, Connecticut

Contents

© Aladdin Books Ltd 1998
Designed and
produced by
Aladdin Books Ltd
28 Percy Street
London W1P 0LD

First published in the United
States in 1998 by
Copper Beech Books,
an imprint of
The Millbrook Press
2 Old New Milford Road
Brookfield, Connecticut
06804

Printed in Belgium
All rights reserved

Editor
Jon Richards
Design
David West
Children's Book Design
Designer
Flick Killerby
Illustrators
Richard Rockwood
& Rob Shone
Picture Research
Brooks Krikler Research

Library Of Congress Cataloging-in-Publication Data
Millard, Anne.
The new book of pharaohs / Anne Millard ; illustrated by Richard Rockwood.
p. cm.
Summary: Explores some of the mysteries surrounding the life and death of King
Tutankhamen and other pharaohs of ancient Egypt.
ISBN 0-7613-0859-8 (lib. bdg.). — ISBN 0-7613-0778-8 (pbk.)
1. Pharaohs—Juvenile literature. [1. Pharaohs.
2. Egypt—Civilization—To 332 B.C. 3. Kings, queens, rulers, etc.]
I. Rockwood, Richard, ill. II. Title.
DT61.M552 1998   98-15579
932—dc21   CIP AC
5 4 3 2 1

INTRODUCTION

Around the time of 3100 B.C., the kingdom of Egypt was united by King Menes. This started the growth of one of the greatest nations ever seen. Over the next 3,000 years, Egypt grew, at one time creating an empire that stretched from Nubia in the south to Palestine in the north. Throughout this land the ancient Egyptians built huge monuments to house their dead and to worship their gods, goddesses, and ancestors. Many of these monuments now lie in ruins, or are hidden completely from view. It is the job of the archaeologist to find these buildings and try to piece them back together so that we can recreate what life may have been like in ancient Egypt.

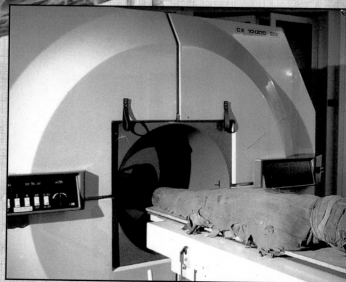

Despite the development of modern technology that allows today's Egyptologists to study monuments and remains in more detail than ever before, there is still no substitute for archaeologists who carefully sift through the shattered and hidden remains. This book examines some of the most recent finds, revealing the latest discoveries as they are unearthed.

Today, archaeologists can use modern technology to help them study the remains of the Egyptian kingdom. *The New Book of Pharaohs* will show some of these modern techniques. These include the use of X rays and CAT scans, which can look inside mummies and coffins without having to open them up and damage them, and the use of cameras with airlocks, which can peer inside tombs without exposing them to the outside air. They have also developed computer programs which, if enough information is fed into them, can recreate just how a monument might have looked in its heyday.

ANCIENT EGYPT

The history of ancient Egypt can be divided into several periods. The first was the Archaic Period (c.3100–2650 B.C.), which was followed by the period known as the Old Kingdom (c.2650–2134 B.C.).

After this there was a brief break called the First Intermediate Period (c.2134–2040 B.C.), and then the Middle Kingdom (c.2040–1640 B.C.), the Second Intermediate Period (c.1640–1550 B.C.), the New Kingdom (c.1550–1070 B.C.), the Third Intermediate Period (c.1070–712 BC), the Late Period (c.712–332 BC), and finally the Greco-Roman Period (c.332 BC – A.D. 395). During these periods, Egypt was ruled by various families, called dynasties. In total there were 32 dynasties, beginning with King Narmer of dynasty 1 and ending with Cleopatra VII of the 32nd dynasty.

CHAPTER ONE
THE LOST TOMB

The deserts of Egypt are rich with the remnants of the ancient kingdom that flourished for nearly 3,500 years. This chapter will show some of the latest archaeological discoveries, and some rediscoveries, from ancient tombs to lost cities.

Particularly rich in remains is the Valley of the Kings. Here, the Egyptians buried their New Kingdom rulers in underground tombs (*see* map *below*). One particular rediscovery in 1987 involved the excavation of the tomb known as KV5. Archaeologists were amazed to discover that the tomb had been built for some of the many sons of Pharaoh Ramses II.

Guide to the Valley of the Kings

A Sons of Ramses II	G Ramses III
B Ramses IX	H Ramses V/VI
C Ramses X	I Tutankhamen
D Sethos I	J Merenptah
E Ramses I	K Ramses II
F Amenmesse	

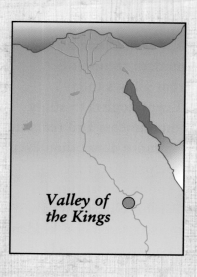

Valley of the Kings

The Valley of the Kings is situated on the west bank of the Nile River opposite the modern city of Luxor (*left*). Some 62 tombs have been discovered so far, including the famous tomb of Tutankhamen (*see* page 15).

Despite its name, the valley does not just include the tombs of kings. A few tombs have been found to contain the remains of favored princes and nobles.

RAMSES THE GREAT

Ramses II, the Great, ruled Egypt between around 1304 –1237 B.C. He was a warrior king who claimed great victories, and was a prolific builder (he built the huge temples at Abu Simbel – *see* pages 18-19). He had several queens, numerous minor wives, and around 200 children! He died an old man, and studies of his mummy (*right*) showed that he suffered from arthritis, heart disease, and tooth decay.

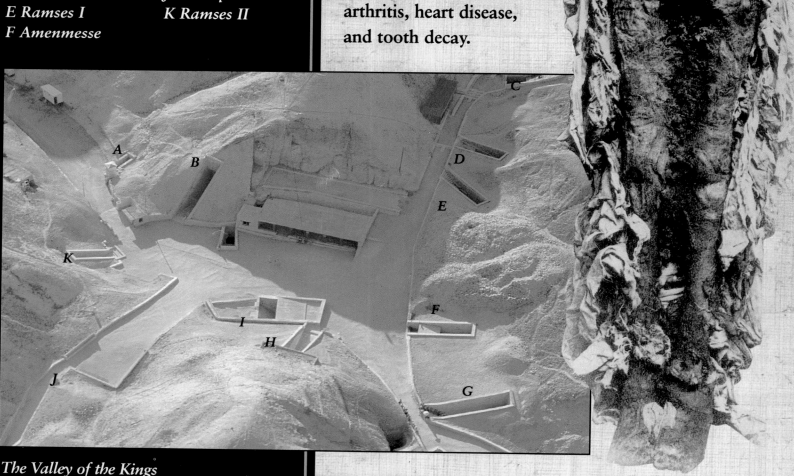

The Valley of the Kings

When the tomb KV5 was opened by Kent Weeks in 1987, it was not for the first time. The tomb was first discovered in the early nineteenth century, but over the years floods had carried tons of sand and rocks into the tomb, filling it almost to the ceiling. People believed it was not worth clearing, the entrance was covered with sand, and the tomb was lost.

KENT WEEKS

Working for the Cairo American University, Professor Kent Weeks (*below*) has been surveying the western bank in order to produce a detailed map of the area. Although tomb KV5 was known about, its exact location remained a mystery. Professor Weeks concentrated his search near the tomb of Ramses IX. However, before he could start he had to persuade souvenir stannd owners to move!

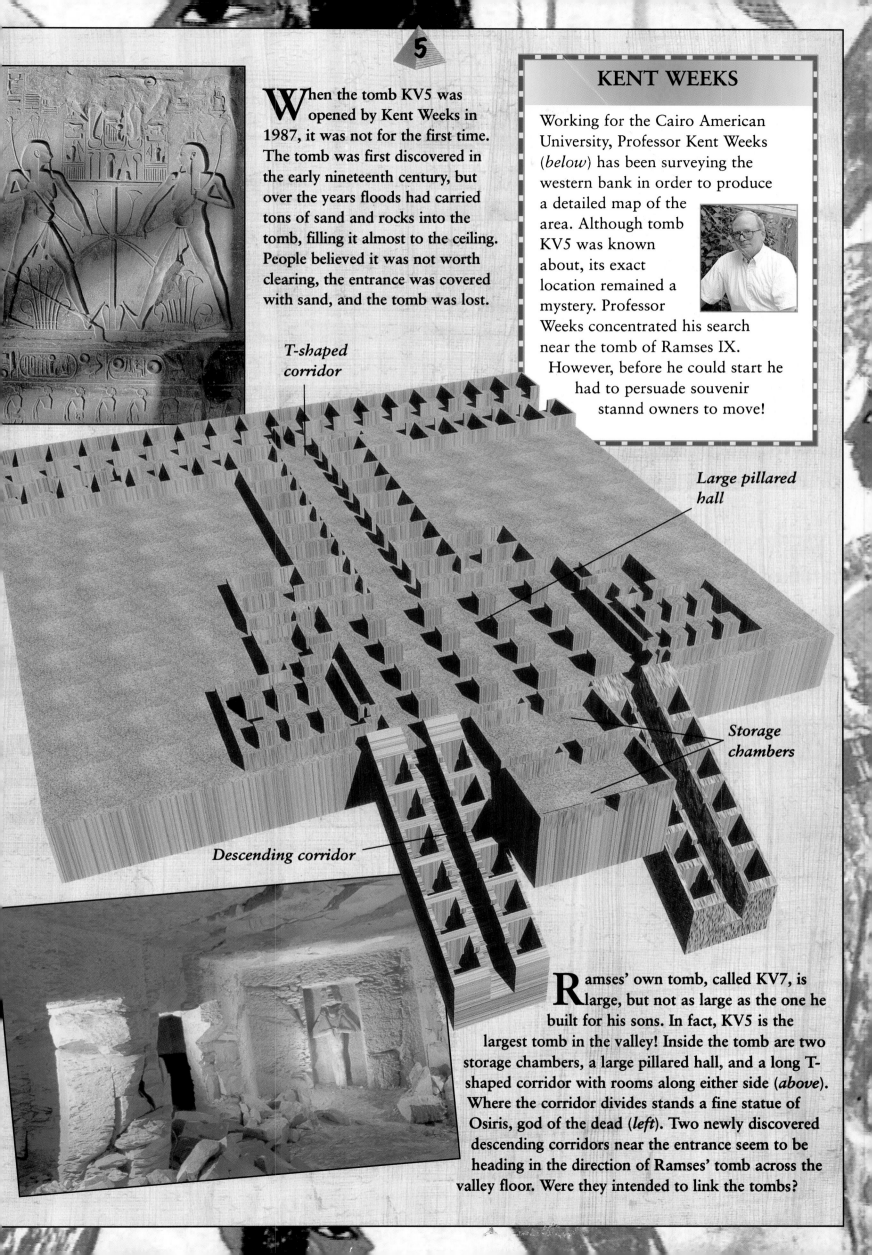

T-shaped corridor

Large pillared hall

Storage chambers

Descending corridor

Ramses' own tomb, called KV7, is large, but not as large as the one he built for his sons. In fact, KV5 is the largest tomb in the valley! Inside the tomb are two storage chambers, a large pillared hall, and a long T-shaped corridor with rooms along either side (*above*). Where the corridor divides stands a fine statue of Osiris, god of the dead (*left*). Two newly discovered descending corridors near the entrance seem to be heading in the direction of Ramses' tomb across the valley floor. Were they intended to link the tombs?

AVARIS, CAPITAL OF THE HYKSOS

By around 1650 B.C., Egypt's great Middle Kingdom (dynasties 11 to 13) had collapsed in chaos. Invaders, who we call Hyksos, had crossed the eastern frontier. "Hyksos" comes from two ancient Egyptian words meaning "rulers of foreign hill countries." Armed with a deadly new weapon – the horse-drawn chariot – they overwhelmed the stunned Egyptians and set up a new state in the delta. They chose a city called Avaris as their capital.

Little was known of these foreign rulers, until an excavation under the control of archaeologist Manfred Bietak found the exact location of Avaris. This on-going expedition has also unearthed many surprising treasures that have revealed some astounding facts about the life of the Hyksos.

There has been much discussion about the location of the Hyksos' capital. Bietak's expedition pinpointed the site to modern-day Tall ad-Dab'a in the Nile Delta (*left*).

Wall paintings found at Avaris appear to show young men and women leaping between the horns of a charging bull (*right*). They amazed archaeologists because of their similarity to wall paintings found at the Palace at Knossos on the island of Crete. The Avaris paintings even appear to be older than those at Knossos. Manfred Bietak also found fragments of paintings, also in the Cretan style, showing plants, trees, acrobats, and hunting scenes.

The paintings at Knossos and Avaris show what archaeologists believe was a bull-leaping ceremony. In it, young acrobats would grab the horns of a bull and somersault over its back (*left*). These acrobats were highly respected for this ritual that may have had some religious purpose.

Cretan bull-leaping ceremony

Discoveries at Avaris have shown how well fortified it was. There were massive walls, 28 feet (8.5 m) thick at the base, and a heavily fortified fortress. After the Hyksos had left, the Egyptians demolished the fortress and built their own that was just as formidable (*left*).

DONKEY BURIALS

Bietak's dig has shown that Avaris was the center of trade with Canaan, Syria, and Crete and many of its inhabitants were Canaanites. Some Canaanites were traders and some graves at Avaris have a pair of donkeys sacrificed at the entrance (*below*) – not an Egyptian custom. Perhaps these men ran the donkey caravans that carried goods to Avaris.

Human skeleton

Donkey skeletons

THE CRETAN CONNECTION

Lying to the north of Egypt, the island of Crete saw the flowering of the Minoan civilization between 1900 and 1400 B.C. The huge palace at Knossos, whose remains can still be seen (*left*), was built around a central courtyard where the bull-leaping ceremony took place. Archaeologists are puzzled about the link between this distant civilization and Egypt. It may be that a Cretan princess married a Hyksos or Egyptian king, who then decorated his palace to remind her of home.

FEUDING FAMILIES

The rulers of ancient Egypt were not without their intrigues or jealous arguments. One such incident involves the New Kingdom Pharaoh Tuthmose III and his attempts to outshine his stepmother, Hatshepsut. Over the past 30 years, archaeologists have been discovering remains that indicate the lengths that Tuthmose III went to in order to better Hatshepsut.

The family tree (*below*) shows how Tuthmose III was Tuthmose II's son by his marriage to one of his other wives, Isis. After Tuthmose II's death, Tuthmose III came to the throne with Hatshepsut acting as regent. However, in a brilliant coup, Hatshepsut replaced Tuthmose III as outright ruler, humiliating the young king. After her death, Tuthmose III set about getting his revenge by defacing her monuments and building his own in order to overshadow hers.

Many aspect of the reign of Queen Hatshepsut (*right*) remained a mystery until the work of Egyptian archaeologist Labib Habachi. He set about piecing together the smashed inscriptions on her monuments and looking at texts from private tombs that date from her reign. The picture that emerged was of a strong ruler who reigned for 15 years, and a powerful warrior who led her troops into battle many times.

WILLFUL DESTRUCTION

After Hatshepsut's death, Thutmose III gave orders to remove all traces of her existence. Her name was cut from her monuments, her pictures chiseled out (*below*), and her statues and inscriptions smashed. The walls of her funeral temple at Deir el Bahari (*see* right) were subject to particular violence. The work of Labib Habachi has shown that these inscriptions portrayed Hatshpesut's achievements, which included her own military victories. In a jealous rage, Tuthmose III had these records destroyed so that they did not overshadow his own conquests.

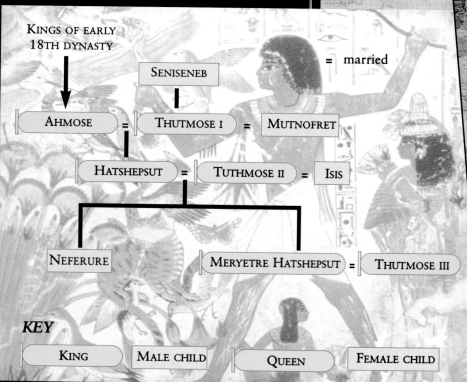

KINGS OF EARLY 18TH DYNASTY

SENISENEB

= married

AHMOSE = THUTMOSE I = MUTNOFRET

HATSHEPSUT = TUTHMOSE II = ISIS

NEFERURE   MERYETRE HATSHEPSUT = THUTMOSE III

KEY

KING   MALE CHILD   QUEEN   FEMALE CHILD

PRIDE BEFORE THE FALL

Though smaller than Hatshepsut's funeral temple (*right*), Thutmose's temple was similar in design, but it was built at a higher level in order to overshadow his stepmother's monument (*below*). However, an earthslide later destroyed his temple, but left hers undamaged.

Temple of Mentuhotep

Temple of Thutmose III

Temple of Hatshepsut

Chapel of the goddess Hathor

THE LOST TEMPLE

In the 1960s, a team of Polish archaeologists began restoring the funeral temple of Hatshepsut. They found blocks from another temple, now totally destroyed, that had belonged to King Thutmose III (*right*). He had built a shrine to the god Amun next to Hatshepsut's funeral temple. All that remains now are broken fragments (*left*), which thousands of tourists ignore as they marvel at the beauty of Hatshepsut's temple!

ABYDOS, THE ROYAL CEMETERY

For many years, archaeologists have disagreed about the location of the final resting place of Egypt's earliest rulers, those from first dynasty. At the turn of the century, the archaeologist Sir William Flinders Petrie found the remains of ten tombs at a site at Abydos in southern Egypt. The tomb stelae were marked with the names of Egypt's earliest kings, so it was assumed that the first dynasty kings were buried in them. However, another archaeologist, Walter Emery, working at Saqqara in the 1930s and 1950s, found much larger tombs bearing the same first dynasty names. He assumed that these were the resting places of the earliest kings. Most recently, an expedition in 1991 discovered boat burials and a series of even larger funeral monuments back at Abydos indicating that the first dynasty kings were, in fact, buried there.

Tomb stela

The 1991 expedition by Pennsylvania and Yale universities uncovered a total of 12 ships that were identical to those used during the first dynasty (*above*). They were 59–69 feet (18–21 m) long and had been placed in shallow trenches and covered in bricks. These boats, like those found by the Giza pyramids (*see* page 29), may have been intended to be used by the king during his afterlife.

THE AFTERLIFE

The Egyptians believed that if they had led virtuous lives, they would be rewarded with eternal happiness. They also believed that they could provide for a comfortable eternity by filling their tombs with their possessions and supplies. However, not all tombs contained actual replicas of possessions and servants. Many had to make do with models of their belongings (*right*).

Burial mounds for household servants

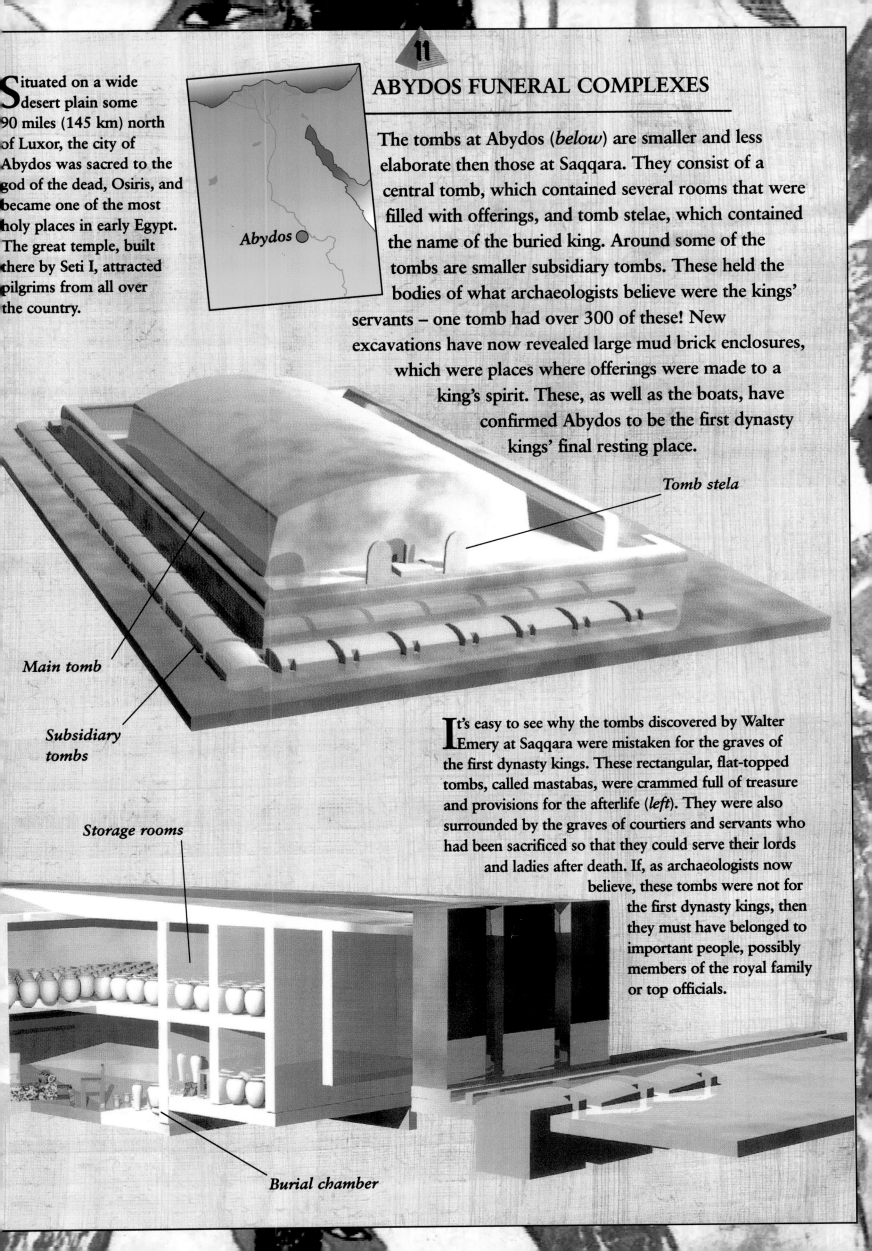

ABYDOS FUNERAL COMPLEXES

Situated on a wide desert plain some 90 miles (145 km) north of Luxor, the city of Abydos was sacred to the god of the dead, Osiris, and became one of the most holy places in early Egypt. The great temple, built there by Seti I, attracted pilgrims from all over the country.

Abydos

The tombs at Abydos (*below*) are smaller and less elaborate then those at Saqqara. They consist of a central tomb, which contained several rooms that were filled with offerings, and tomb stelae, which contained the name of the buried king. Around some of the tombs are smaller subsidiary tombs. These held the bodies of what archaeologists believe were the kings' servants – one tomb had over 300 of these! New excavations have now revealed large mud brick enclosures, which were places where offerings were made to a king's spirit. These, as well as the boats, have confirmed Abydos to be the first dynasty kings' final resting place.

Tomb stela

Main tomb

Subsidiary tombs

Storage rooms

It's easy to see why the tombs discovered by Walter Emery at Saqqara were mistaken for the graves of the first dynasty kings. These rectangular, flat-topped tombs, called mastabas, were crammed full of treasure and provisions for the afterlife (*left*). They were also surrounded by the graves of courtiers and servants who had been sacrificed so that they could serve their lords and ladies after death. If, as archaeologists now believe, these tombs were not for the first dynasty kings, then they must have belonged to important people, possibly members of the royal family or top officials.

Burial chamber

The Tombs of Saqqara

Even though archaeologists believe that it does not hold the bodies of Egypt's earliest kings, there is little doubt about Saqqara's importance as a cemetery – its position on the edge of the desert and its location near to the ancient capital of Memphis saw to that. Almost everybody was buried there, from later kings and queens, through great officials and the middle classes, right down to the humblest peasants. As well as the early mastaba tombs (*see* page 11), archaeologists have recently discovered the tombs of top-ranking officials from the reign of the boy-king, Tutankhamen, including his treasurer and one of his generals. They have also found a great number of mummified animals that were buried in underground galleries that riddle the ground beneath the area. These animal corpses were said to contain the spirits of gods and goddesses.

Saqqara is found some 13 miles (20 km) south of Cairo.

TOMB DECORATIONS

Once the insides of the tombs had been cleared of rubble (*above*), they revealed an unusual sight. Maya and his wife Merit had superb, golden-yellow paintings in theirs, while other tombs at Saqqara were not normally decorated.

ANIMAL MUMMIES

Once, whole species of animals were honored as containers for the spirits of gods on Earth. Work at Saqqara by the Egypt Excavation Society (EES) has revealed that they embalmed and buried countless hawks, baboons, cats, and ibises. The ibises were placed in huge underground galleries that run for great distances. The picture (*below*) shows Professor Emery of the EES entering one of these galleries.

A mummified baboon

Entrance to the animal galleries

The courtyards above Horemheb's tomb (*below*) were lined with decorated limestone slabs. They record his career as a general during the reigns of the kings Akhenaton and Tutankhamen (*see* pages 22-25). Horemheb (shown *right* making offerings to the goddess Hathor) later seized the throne, so he was buried in the Valley of the Kings. Excavations of his underground tomb complex began in 1975. After clearing the complicated series of twisting passages, chambers, and halls, they found the remains of Horemheb's second wife, Queen Mutnodjmet.

Maya's underground tomb

Horemheb's underground tomb

THE TOMB OF TUTANKHAMEN'S TREASURER

The discovery of both Horemheb's and Maya's tomb was overseen by Professor Geoffrey Martin working for the EES and the Lieden Museum of the Netherlands. Like the tomb of Horemheb, Maya's consisted of a maze of long, twisting corridors buried beneath a structure that resembled a small temple, complete with a ceremonial gateway (called a pylon), an open courtyard, and a chapel (*above*). Work on clearing Maya's tomb started in 1987. The unique tomb decorations of golden-yellow paint (*see far left*), traditionally the color of resurrection, indicate the importance of Maya (*left*). During his life he worked as Tutankhamen's treasury official.

CHAPTER TWO
FINDING PHARAOHS

This chapter will look at how archaeologists have made some of their discoveries and what techniques are being used today to find, preserve, and even rebuild some of these ancient monuments.

Although Egypt's monuments date back over 5,000 years, it has only been in the last 200 that interest in the ancient empire has grown. In 1798, Napoléon's army traveled with a group of scholars who recorded many of the monuments. Their "Description of Egypt" helped arouse a fever of interest in Egypt. With many early tourists eager to buy antiquities as souvenirs, many Egyptians were encouraged to rob and sell their own heritage. Some of those who "officially" dug sites were not much better. One explorer even blasted his way into a pyramid with dynamite! Since then, fortunately, digging techniques have improved and the acquisition of antiquities is subject to tighter controls.

HIEROGLYPHS

About 5,000 years ago, the Egyptians invented a form of picture writing called hieroglyphs. Over time, their meanings were lost and they remained a mystery until the discovery in 1799 of a stone fragment near Rosetta in the Nile Delta (*above right*). It contained writings in hieroglyphs, demotic (a form of Egyptian writing), and Greek. Using this, the French scholar, Jean-François Champollion was able to work out how to read the hieroglyphs.

The first tourists were the ancient Egyptians themselves, interested in their already ancient past. But in the Late Period, when Egypt's power had declined, they started reviving old texts, art styles, and cults, hoping this would restore Egypt's ancient glories. Then came Greek and Roman tourists, who ranked the pyramids at Giza (*see* pages 28-29) and the lighthouse at Alexandria (*see* pages 16-17) as two of the Seven Wonders of the World. Interest waned for many years until the late 18th century, when foreign explorers and collectors started to discover and explore the ancient sites (*below*)!

MODERN EXCAVATIONS

Modern excavations involve careful scientific research (*above*). They use the latest technology, including the use of sonar (*below*), to discover and record new remains. The aim is not just to find beautiful objects, but to learn everything we can about how the ancient Egyptians lived, what they did, how and why they did it, and what they felt and believed.

DISCOVERING TUTANKHAMEN

The most famous discovery of ancient Egyptian remains was that of the tomb of Tutankhamen. The entrance to the tomb was uncovered in 1922 by the English achaeologist Howard Carter, and over the next few years, the tomb gave up a treasure trove of artifacts, including beds, chairs, bows and arrows, and trumpets (one of which was even played some years later at the Cairo Museum). But perhaps the greatest discovery inside the tomb were the coffins of the king. Most amazing was the third coffin, which was made from 296 pounds (110 kg) of solid gold!

UNDERWATER TREASURES

Excavating remains is difficult under normal conditions. But when they lie submerged on the seabed, it makes things a lot harder. Archaeologists have to cope with shifting water currents, as well as not being able to breathe without the help of special equipment. This equipment has only been developed in recent years, and with it archaeologists are retrieving remains that were once thought lost forever. These include the remains of part of a city of the ancient world. Founded by Alexander the Great in 331 B.C., Alexandria grew to become one of the greatest cities in the Mediterranean world. It declined in late Roman times, and, after the Arabs founded Cairo, Alexandria was neglected. Earthquakes caused some buildings to collapse and slip into the sea, while others simply crumbled. Here they remained until 1994, when a team of French and Egyptian divers started bringing pieces to the surface.

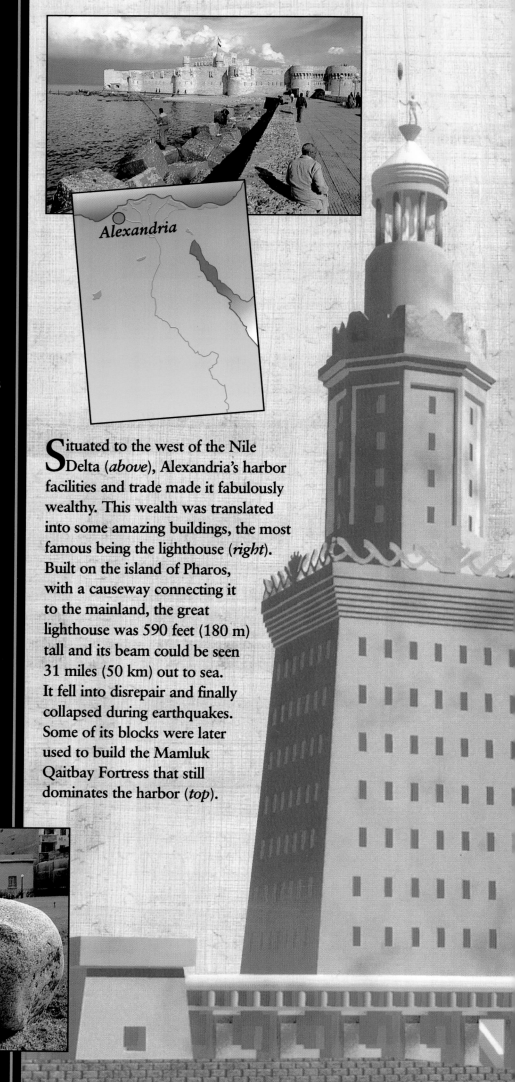

Alexandria

Situated to the west of the Nile Delta (*above*), Alexandria's harbor facilities and trade made it fabulously wealthy. This wealth was translated into some amazing buildings, the most famous being the lighthouse (*right*). Built on the island of Pharos, with a causeway connecting it to the mainland, the great lighthouse was 590 feet (180 m) tall and its beam could be seen 31 miles (50 km) out to sea. It fell into disrepair and finally collapsed during earthquakes. Some of its blocks were later used to build the Mamluk Qaitbay Fortress that still dominates the harbor (*top*).

Granite statue retrieved from the seabed.

CLEOPATRA

For much of the Late Period (c.712–332 B.C.), Egypt was under the rule of a succession of foreign kings and queens, including Nubians, Assyrians, and Persians. Then came the Ptolemies, who were descended from General Ptolemy, a commander under Alexander the Great in the army that conquered Egypt in 332 B.C. Perhaps the most famous of these was Cleopatra VII. She used her cunning to woo the Roman generals Julius Caeser and Marc Antony. In doing so she greatly improved Egypt's standing in the world. However, she also succeeded in annoying many back in Rome. In the end, Rome invaded and conquered Egypt. Cleopatra committed suicide, and Egypt lost its independence, falling under the direct rule of Rome.

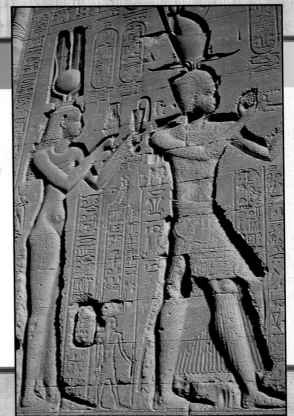

WORKING UNDERWATER

The lighthouse of Alexandria

The remains of ancient Alexandria were first discovered on the floor of the harbor in 1916. During the 1960s, Egyptian archaeologist Kamal Abu el Sadat discovered huge statues among the rubble. Things eventually came to a head when plans were announced for a concrete breakwater to sit over the area where the statues had been spotted. Archaeologists began to work quickly to retrieve as much of the ancient city as they could. During the underwater investigation of the site, divers painstakingly mapped out the remains, plotting the positions of the main pieces so that they could be brought up later (*below*). Using computers and specially designed software, the archaeologists could plot the positions of the remains to within 4–12 inches (10–30 cm). So far, some 34 large statues, including this pink granite bust (*left*), and pieces of buildings have been raised.

Diving archaeologists lifting remains from an underwater site.

SAVING HISTORY

After surviving earthquakes, floods, and other natural disasters for thousands of years, Egypt's remaining monuments are now under the threat of increasing human interference. In 1960, the United Nations Educational, Scientific, and Cultural Organisation (UNESCO) launched a campaign to study the sites in Nubia to the south of Egypt, a province of the empire. These sites were in danger of being drowned when the Aswan Dam was built, forming Lake Nasser behind it. A total of 23 temples were taken down and rebuilt elsewhere. Some even left the country! The temple of Dendut was given to the United States in gratitude for its help during the enormous project.

Other threats include vandalism (many sites are covered with graffiti, *below*), while others are simply crumbling due to the millions of tourists who walk through them year after year.

A MAMMOTH MOVE

Three thousand years ago, Ramses II built two spectacular rock-cut temples at Abu Simbel in Nubia to honor three gods, one goddess, and himself and his queen, Nefertari. Rather than leave them to drown beneath the rising waters of Lake Nasser, the temples were carved into huge blocks and moved to artificial mounds above the waters of the lake (*below*).

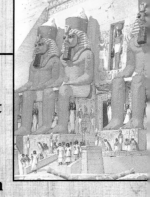

Another monument was the temple of Isis at Philae (*left*). Already partially drowned by an earlier dam, the temple was carefully dismantled and rebuilt on a nearby island.

Artificial mounds

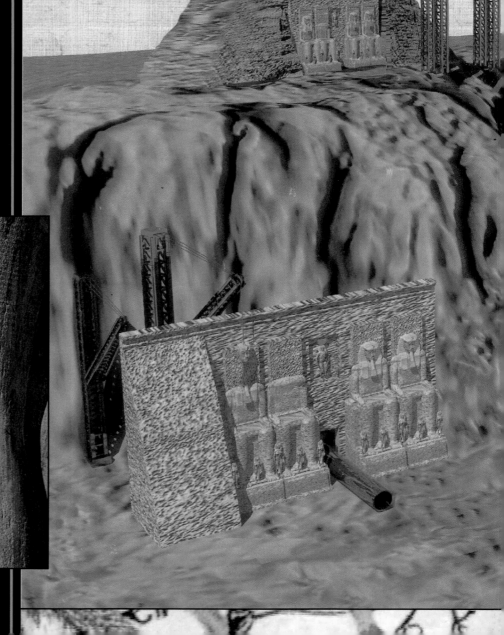

Over the years, the Sphinx at Giza has suffered the impact of the elements and humans. At one time it was even used as an artillery target! Today, the main threat comes from the weather. Salt discovered in the mortar was eating away at the statue. Over a period of ten years, the statue was repaired (*below*) and a new covering of limestone was added to protect the core. The renovated Sphinx was revealed in 1998.

BEFORE AND AFTER

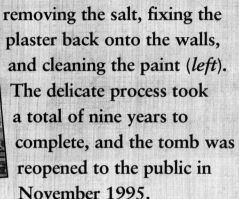

After its discovery in the Valley of the Queens in 1904, the staggeringly beautiful tomb of Queen Nefertari began to deteriorate rapidly and had to be closed. Sweating visitors had made the air so damp that salt crystals emerged, peeling the paint off the walls! The Getty Conservation Institute and the Egyptian Antiquities Service embarked on the slow, delicate work of removing the salt, fixing the plaster back onto the walls, and cleaning the paint (*left*). The delicate process took a total of nine years to complete, and the tomb was reopened to the public in November 1995.

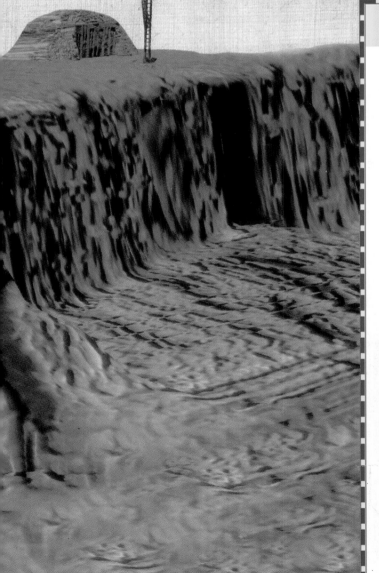

TOURISM

Every year, around 3 million people visit Egypt to gaze at the impressive monuments left by its ancient empire. While bringing much needed money into Egypt, the sheer numbers of people attracted to the sites can have disastrous consequences. Millions of pairs of feet can wear away paths, people brush up against fragile paintings and carvings, and the breath of thousands of tourists can damage delicate remains beyond repair (*see above*). Some sites have had to be closed because of the damage that they have suffered, but rather than leave them shut permanently, archaeologists have started the painstaking process of repairing these sites to their former glory.

Rebuilding the Past

REBUILDING THE PAST

With the help of modern science, archaeologists can now learn a great deal more than their predecessors could have, both about sites and the objects found in them. X rays and CAT scans can look inside mummies without having to unwrap them. Planes and hot-air balloons let archaeologists get a bird's-eye view of the countryside to spot any buried buildings. Scientists can remove microscopic parts of ancient bodies and examine them to find out who was related to whom (*see right*).

The advent of powerful computers has also allowed archaeologists the chance to rebuild the past. Using their knowlegde of the shattered remnants that litter Egypt, they can recreate monuments, allowing computer-generated pyramids to rise from the ground. They can even rebuild the faces of the Egyptian rulers, allowing us to gaze into the eyes of these once-powerful people.

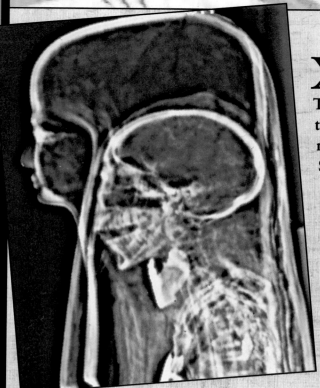

X rays are rays of light that we cannot see. They have so much energy that they can pass through many solid objects. Scientists can use special types of photographic film to record what these X rays pass through and what they don't. The result is a picture of the inside of an object. In this case, the skeleton of a mummy can be seen inside a coffin (*left*).

GENE BANK

Inside every cell of our bodies is a long stringlike substance that governs what we look like. It is called deoxyribonucleic acid, or DNA (*right*). Scientists can remove DNA from a mummy and find out which family it came from by comparing it with DNA from other mummies. It has been decided to set up an ancient Egyptian DNA bank, using all the Egyptian mummies in museums across the world.

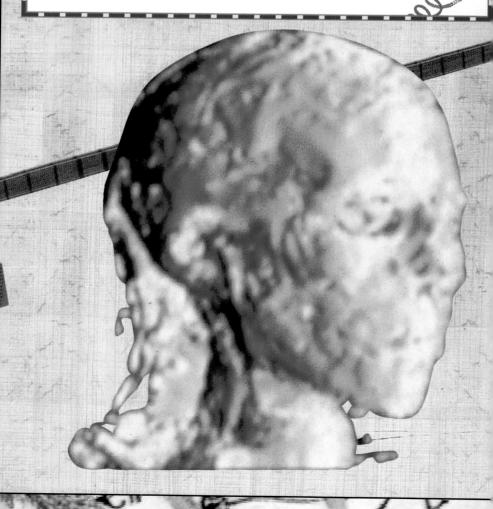

COMPUTER RECONSTRUCTION

If you can feed enough measurements and details into a computer, the process known as computer-aided design (CAD) can "rebuild" a ruined building for you. For some 30 years, French scholars have been working at Saqqara on the ruined pyramid complex of Pepi I, a king of the sixth dynasty who reigned some 4,300 years ago. Their mass of data has been used in a CAD of the pyramid and its mortuary temple (*below*), allowing us to appreciate the original splendor of this now-ruined monument.

Buried buildings cannot usually be seen from the ground, but they become visible from the air. As this picture of the Workman's Village (*above*) shows, the outlines of buildings are easy to spot on the desert floor near the Valley of the Kings. Flying over the countryside and taking photographs has become standard practice. A hot air balloon has been recently used for aerial photography for both the Amarna dig and the survey of the west bank at Thebes.

Pepi I's pyramid

Mortuary temple

Queen's pyramids

FACE FROM THE PAST

A coaxial tomagraphy (CAT) scanner (*right*) is a special kind of X-ray machine. It takes slice-like images through an object without the need to open the object up and damage it. Scientists can then manipulate these "slices" and build three-dimensional views of the whole object.

Despite the attempts of the ancient Egyptians to preserve their dead, many corpses have deteriorated to the extent that all that is left is a skeleton. Nevertheless, scientists can reconstruct the faces of these corpses using either modelling clay or computers. Scientists can recreate the muscles by examining the attachment points where they joined the bone. Finally, the thickness of the flesh can be calculated and skin can be added using the computer or clay to complete the face, letting us see the face of somebody who has been dead for thousands of years (*left*).

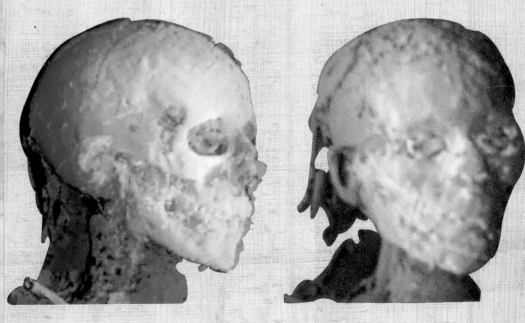

CHAPTER THREE
THE LOST WIFE

Egypt's monuments do more than just provide us with amazing beauty. They also tell us a great deal about how the ancient Egyptians lived. This chapter will examine how the latest discoveries have solved many mysteries about Egyptian life and, in particular, the arrangements of Egyptian royalty, including mystery wives, intermarriage, and even a royal murder!

One important mystery involves the 14th-century-B.C. king, Akhenaton. Inscriptions from the early part of his reign show that he was devoted to his wife, Nefertiti. However, recently found evidence shows that there was a second woman in his life, referred to as his "Dearly Beloved Wife, Kiya." The revelation that Kiya had a tomb in the Valley of the Kings shows that this mystery wife was very important. She may also have been the mother of Akhenaton's heir, Tutankhamen.

Inside tomb KV55, archaeologists found a beautiful coffin (*left*). However, the coffin was unable to reveal any clues as to the identity of the body it contained. The inscriptions that would have borne the name of the person inside had been deliberately hacked away. It is now thought that the coffin belonged to Kiya at one time, but archaeologists are still unsure whose body was inside when it was found.

As well as the beautiful coffin, tomb KV55 contained four special containers called canopic jars (*left*). Topped with stoppers shaped like human heads, these jars contained the internal organs of the mummy, such as the intestines and the liver. These had been removed from the body and carefully preserved.

THE MYSTERY TOMB

In 1907, a tomb in the Valley of the Kings, labeled KV55, was discovered by an American businessman, Theodore Davis. He set about clearing the tomb very quickly. A little too quickly, as many of the artefacts were damaged and even destroyed in the clearance. Davis noted that during the removal of the mummy "the front teeth fell into the dust when touched." But who was in the tomb? Originally it was believed that the tomb was built for Akhenaton's mother, Queen Tiy. However, further examination of the mummy suggests that the body was that of a man, but exactly who still remains a mystery.

When Akhenaton died, he was succeeded by his son, Tutankhamen, whose mother, many archaeologists believe, was Kiya. When he came to the throne, Tutankhamen was about eight years old and so had regents to rule for him. As was the custom, he married his half sister, Ankhesenamen (*see bottom*). In all, Tutankhamen only reigned for nine years and examinations of his skeleton indicate that his life may have ended abruptly.

X rays of his skull (*below*) suggest that his death may have been a murder, caused by a blow to the back of the head!

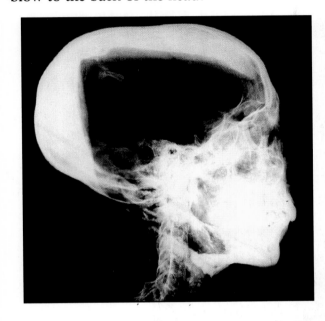

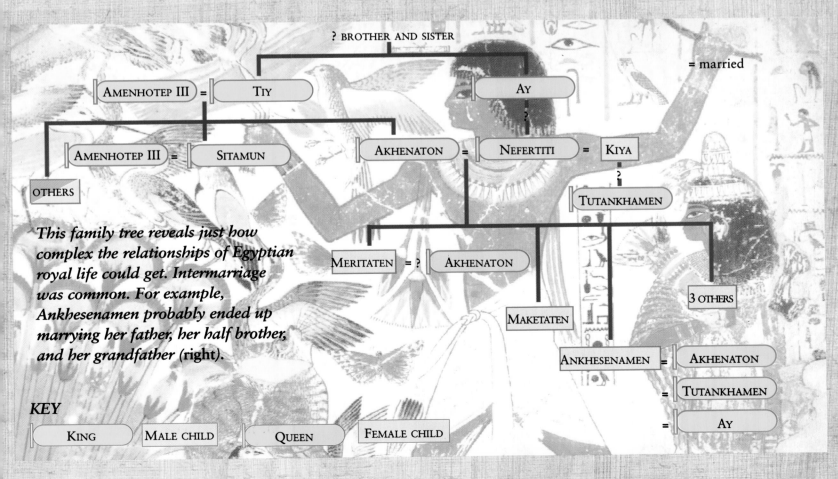

? BROTHER AND SISTER

= married

AMENHOTEP III = TIY

AY

AMENHOTEP III = SITAMUN

AKHENATON = NEFERTITI = KIYA

OTHERS

TUTANKHAMEN

This family tree reveals just how complex the relationships of Egyptian royal life could get. Intermarriage was common. For example, Ankhesenamen probably ended up marrying her father, her half brother, and her grandfather (right).

MERITATEN = ? AKHENATON

3 OTHERS

MAKETATEN

ANKHESENAMEN = AKHENATON

= TUTANKHAMEN

= AY

KEY

KING   MALE CHILD   QUEEN   FEMALE CHILD

THE FEMALE KING

The reign of Akhenaton was unique. He abandoned many of the traditional ways of Egypt, adopting a new religion and building a new capital city at Amarna (*see* pages 26-27). After his reign, Egypt returned to its traditional ways, branding Akhenaton a heretic and demolishing his temples. The rubble from these ruins was then used in the foundations of other buildings. Archaeologists have been discovering these shattered remains for over 70 years. However, they have only recently begun the process of piecing them together, like an enormous jigsaw puzzle, to rebuild Akhenaton's shattered monuments. From them they have learned a lot about his reign and have been able to answer many questions about his reign, including a new role for his favorite wife, Nefertiti (*below*).

A NEW RELIGION

After rejecting many of Egypt's traditions, Akhenaton created a new religion, around an old sun god, Aten. The most commonly used symbol for Aten was the sun disk with rays of light coming from it (*below*). However, the new religion was short lived, and after Akhenaton's death Egypt returned to its old religion, his new capital city was deserted, and his temples were demolished.

One of the Aten shrines built by Akhenaton at Karnak was for Nefertiti's use alone. The focus of the shrine was a huge pillared courtyard decorated only with female figures (right). As with many of Akhenaton's monuments, this shrine was demolished after his reign.

After the 12th year of Akhenaton's reign, references to Nefertiti (*left*) stop. Archaeologists believed that she had fallen out of favor. However, a recent theory based on inscriptions from demolished temples indicate that Akhenaton may have made her his coruler. She effectively became a king, ruling by his side for the rest of his reign. She may also have outlived him. If so, she died early in Tutankhamen's reign.

Another unique aspect of Akhenaton's reign was the way the royal family was portrayed on monuments. Statues show them with swollen bellies and stretched heads, and reliefs show his family in quite intimate scenes. He is shown playing, kissing, and hugging his children (*right*), and in one scene he and Nefertiti are openly mourning the death of one of their daughters.

Pieces of Akhenaton's temples found at Karnak.

THE AMARNA TEMPLE PROJECT

Archaeologists found over 35,000 blocks (*left*) from four dismantled shrines that Akhenaton had built at Karnak. These blocks had been reused, but hidden inside other buildings. The blocks were numbered and the details of the pictures on them were recorded on computer. Scholars could then start matching blocks and build up scenes like a gigantic jigsaw puzzle, showing what the original pictures and buildings looked like.

LIVING IN THE CITY

The Nile River played a central role in Egyptian life. People were, and still are, dependent on its waters to irrigate crops and provide them with food. So when the pharaoh Akhenaton moved his capital city, he chose a site on the eastern bank of the Nile, at the site of the modern-day town of Amarna. The city, which he called Akhetaton, was situated on a small plain, with cliffs behind it to the east and the river on the west.

Excavations at Amarna, as well as other sites, have told historians a lot about town and village life in ancient Egypt. They have been able to build up a picture of crowded, noisy, and cramped streets with close-packed houses. Inside these buildings the Egyptians carried out their jobs, including rearing livestock, weaving cloth, and even brewing their own beer!

THE NEW CITY

Akhenaton's new capital city at Amarna was a beautiful place of palaces and temples with more modest houses, granaries (*left*), and workplaces in between (*below*). It was abandoned after his death, and much of it now lies under modern fields. Recent excavations have changed our ideas of the layout of some of these village houses (*see below*).

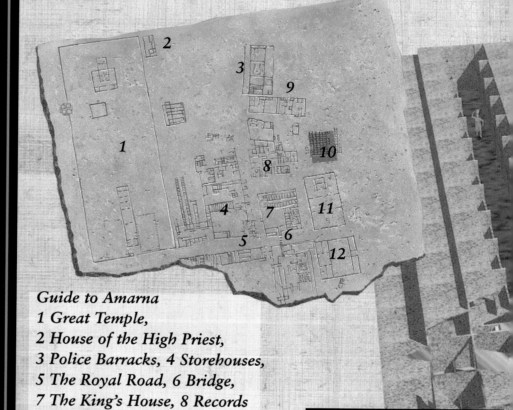

Guide to Amarna
1 Great Temple,
2 House of the High Priest,
3 Police Barracks, 4 Storehouses,
5 The Royal Road, 6 Bridge,
7 The King's House, 8 Records Office, 9 Military Headquarters,
10 Housing, 11 Smaller Temple,
12 Great Pillared Hall

The Nile River

Memphis

Amarna

Baking was important in Egyptian life. This statue shows a woman carrying a basket of bread on her head.

CLUTTERED HOUSING

The excavations at Amarna and at Memphis (*left*) farther down the Nile, as well as models and paintings on the walls of tombs, show that normal housing in ancient Egypt's towns and villages was usually packed tightly together. Because land was scarce, some houses had as many as four stories. They were built next to each other along narrow streets (*below*).

Two-story housing

Narrow street

Village walls

TUTANKHAMEN'S DRINK

Everyone in ancient Egypt, from pharaoh to peasant, drank beer. During the recent excavations at Amarna, archaeologists found widespread evidence of beer making. Ancient beer took about four days to make and was drunk immediately. It was made in many strengths, flavors, and colors. Brewers in the United Kingdom have recently used methods and ingredients noted from tomb paintings to brew a modern version of this ancient Egyptian beer (*left*).

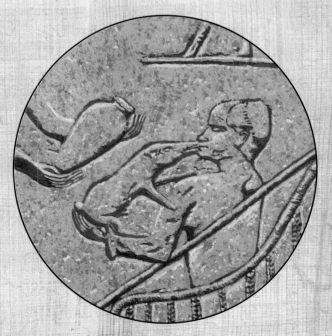

Ancient Egyptians apparently loved roast pork. The recent Amarna dig, started in 1977 and continuing today, has shown that the people in the village had a hobby – they were breeding and fattening pigs on an impressive scale! This inscription (*above*) shows a man weaning a young pig.

BUILDING THE PYRAMIDS

The pyramids at Giza (*see bottom*) have attracted so much study and excavation, you would think there was nothing left to find. Over the last ten years, however, archaeologists have made a variety of important new discoveries. These have included a second funeral boat, paved roads linking the pyramids to quarries, a town for priests and officials who served the pyramid, and a cemetery for dead workers. They have also discovered housing for the twenty to thirty thousand workers that lived nearby at any one time, as well as buildings dedicated to feeding, clothing, and looking after their needs, including a bakery and a place where fish were dried and stored for meals. All of these discoveries have given scholars a peek into the organization behind one of the largest building projects ever undertaken.

EARTHQUAKE!

This picture highlights one of the problems faced by Egypt's monuments. Taken by an Austrian tourist in 1992, it shows stones, dust, and debris tumbling down the side of the step pyramid at Saqqara. The dust and debris were dislodged by an earthquake.

Many other monuments have been completely destroyed by earthquakes and landslides, including Tuthmose III's temple (*see* page 9).

THE WORKFORCE

The pyramids were NOT built by slaves, but by a permanent force of skilled stonemasons, plus an army of laborers who hauled the stones. Since money had not yet been invented, taxes were paid in goods and labor. The stonehaulers were ordinary peasants, paying their labor-tax to the king. During their three-month stint, the king fed, clothed, and housed them. The men were divided into gangs. A gang would load a stone block on to a sledge, then haul it up a ramp into place (*right*).

GIZA

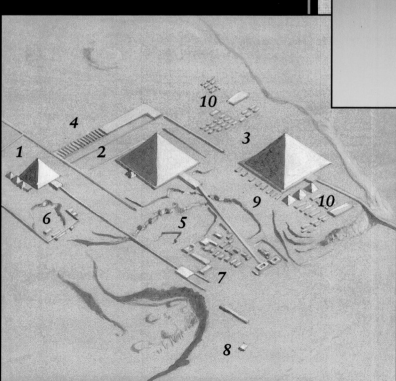

The pyramid complex at Giza

1 Menkhare's pyramid, 2 Khafre's pyramid,
3 Khufu's pyramid, 4 Khafre's workshops,
5 Khufu's quarry, 6 Menkhare's quarry,
7 Khentkawe's town, 8 Bakery site,
9 Possible ramp site and Khafre's quarry,
10 Mastaba tombs.

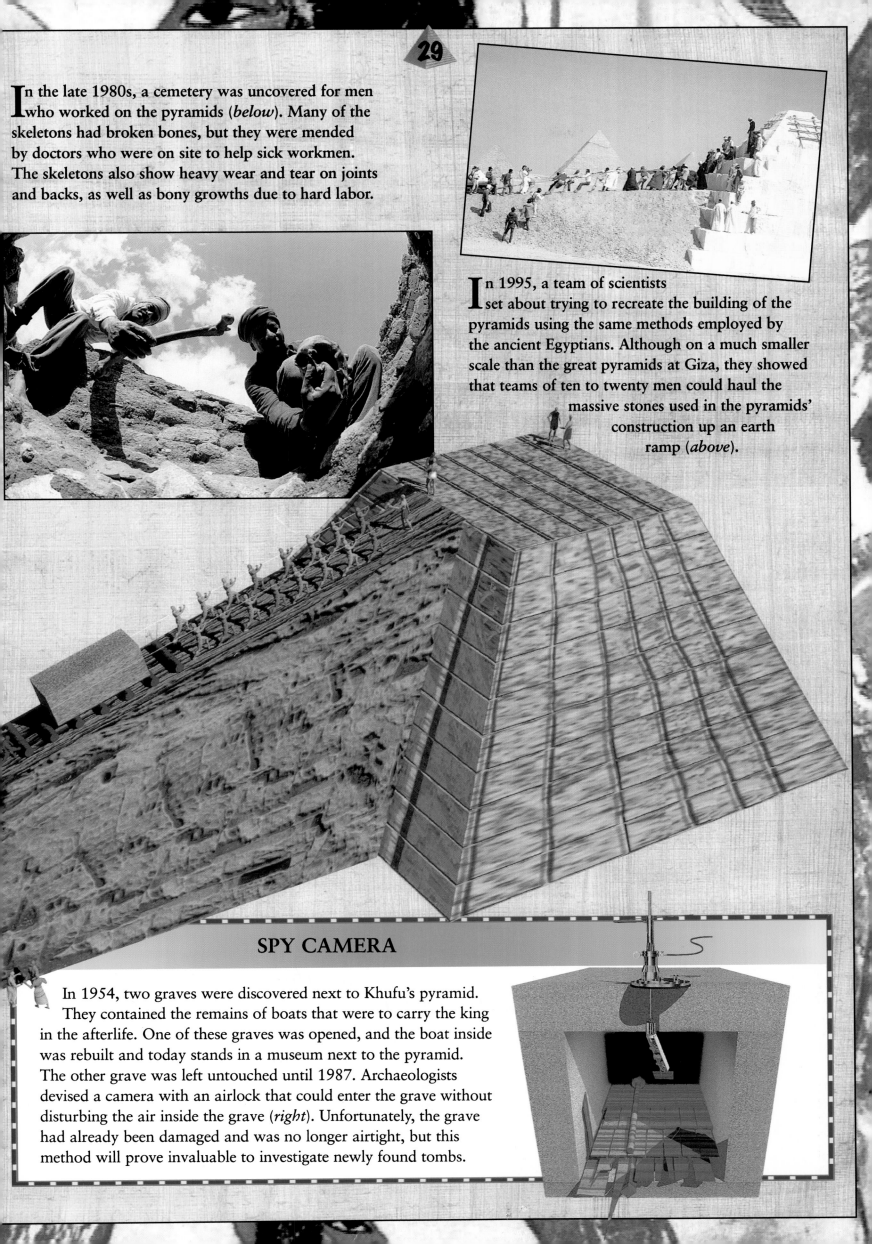

In the late 1980s, a cemetery was uncovered for men who worked on the pyramids (*below*). Many of the skeletons had broken bones, but they were mended by doctors who were on site to help sick workmen. The skeletons also show heavy wear and tear on joints and backs, as well as bony growths due to hard labor.

In 1995, a team of scientists set about trying to recreate the building of the pyramids using the same methods employed by the ancient Egyptians. Although on a much smaller scale than the great pyramids at Giza, they showed that teams of ten to twenty men could haul the massive stones used in the pyramids' construction up an earth ramp (*above*).

SPY CAMERA

In 1954, two graves were discovered next to Khufu's pyramid. They contained the remains of boats that were to carry the king in the afterlife. One of these graves was opened, and the boat inside was rebuilt and today stands in a museum next to the pyramid. The other grave was left untouched until 1987. Archaeologists devised a camera with an airlock that could enter the grave without disturbing the air inside the grave (*right*). Unfortunately, the grave had already been damaged and was no longer airtight, but this method will prove invaluable to investigate newly found tombs.

Glossary & TIMELINE

Abydos
Egyptian city that was sacred to Osiris, the god of the dead. Archaeologists believe it to be the resting place of the earliest Egyptian kings.

Alexandria
City on the Mediterranean coast, founded by Alexander the Great, the Macedonian king who conquered Egypt. The city contained an impressive library and a huge lighthouse that was one of The Seven Wonders of the Ancient World.

Amarna
The site of the city of Akhenaton, one the of ancient capitals of Egypt, founded by the pharaoh Akhenaton.

Archaeologist
A person who uncovers and studies historical remains.

Canopic jars
Small jars that were used to hold the intestines of a dead body after they had been removed during mummification.

Hieroglyphs
A form of ancient Egyptian writing that uses small pictures instead of letters.

Hyksos
A people of unknown origin who settled in the Nile Delta and ruled Egypt from their capital Avaris. Their name comes from two ancient Egyptian words meaning "rulers of foreign hill countries."

Mastaba
From the Arabic for "bench," mastabas are rectangular buildings that cover the tombs of some of Egypt's earliest kings and nobles.

Memphis
The capital of Egypt for almost 400 years, it lies on the west bank of the Nile just south of the modern-day capital, Cairo.

1960 Temples at Abu Simbel dismantled and moved.

1799 Rosetta Stone is discovered.

Mummy
The preserved remains of a dead person. Egyptian mummies were either preserved naturally by the drying-out effects of the sand, or artificially by using natron, salt that was used as a drying agent during the process of mummification.

1998 Renovation of the Sphinx completed.

1954 Boat is discovered next to the pyramids at Giza.

1922 Howard Carter discovers the tomb of Tutankhamen.

Nile
The river that flows through the Egypt. Its waters were, and still are, vital to Egypt, watering the crops along its banks.

Osiris
The ancient Egyptian god and king of the dead.

Pharaoh
A title used by the rulers of Egypt from the Amarna period onward. It comes from the name for a royal palace, the "per-aa," or Great House.

Regent
A person who effectively rules for the monarch. This is because the monarch is too young to rule in person. In ancient Egypt, for example, Hatshepsut acted as regent for the young King Tuthmose III.

Saqqara
Found on the edge of the desert, Saqqara was an important site as it was used as a cemetery throughout the period of ancient Egypt.

Stela
An inscribed stone slab. Those placed in or near tombs act as memorials to the dead and pray for food and drink in the next world.

Temple
A building constructed for the worship of a god or goddess.

Tomb
A room or building constructed to hold the body of a dead person. The Egyptians built underground tombs, tombs cut into cliffs and huge pyramids to hold the bodies of their rulers and nobles.

UNESCO
The United Nations Educational, Scientific, and Cultural Organization. This organization was responsible for the relocation of 23 temples away from the rising waters of Lake Nasser.

Valley of the Kings
Found on the west bank of the Nile, opposite the modern town of Luxor, this valley contains the bodies of the kings from the New Kingdom, as well as some of their families and associates.

Valley of the Queens
Found next to the Valley of the Kings, this valley was used for the burial of queens and royal children from the 19th and 20th dynasties.

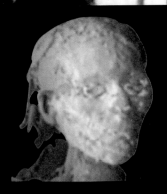

Index